Current issues in public sector management

Peat Marwick
1 Puddle Dock, Blackfriars, London EC4V 3PD
Telephone: 01-236 8000
Telex: 8811541 PMM LON G
Telefax: 01-248 6552 (Group 3)
DX 38050 Blackfriars

ISBN: 1 85061 069 X

Printed in the UK by Bourne Press Limited

Contents

Introduction

The aim of this book is to describe and analyse what has been happening in the management of the public sector since the start of 1984. Our audience is the lay person who has not been immersed in the subject of public administration. We hope he or she will be interested in a field of management that is little discussed.

Our earlier book, *Financial Management in the Public Sector 1979-1984*, introduced the large number of changes which the Thatcher administration had set in hand. The scale of change has, if anything, increased. In central departments there has been a plethora of new initiatives covering performance-related pay, purchasing and office accommodation as well as continuing pressures from the Financial Management Initiative. Rayner scrutinies have been repackaged to maintain their impetus and focus more on making recommended changes happen. Local government officers have been equally subject to changing conventions and processes. Floods of reports from the Audit Commission require action, while legislative proposals on buses, airports and competitive tendering threaten major upheavals in roles and organisation. In the health service the calls for change from Salmon, Griffiths, Ceri Davies and Körner reach every corner of every authority and even call into question the role and performance of each clinician.

One obvious question must be whether managers can adopt and implement so much so quickly. Is there not a risk that the human aspects of change—particularly where the use of advanced technology is concerned—will slow down effective implementation? There is certainly evidence that some initial timetables for jumbo computer projects have been too optimistic. Skills shortages are hindering the achievement of some FMI targets. In the NHS some of the targets set centrally by the Körner committee look particularly unlikely.

A further feature is that some of the managerial messages are becoming deadened through frequent repetition. 'Must efficiency be boring' asked a memorable *Times* editorial at the time of the July 1984 White Paper on the FMI. If worthy but dull edicts flow in a regular stream, managers will soon formalise and institutionalise their responses. A way has to be found of asking the same question in another way or from a different perspective. Sadly, value for money and FMI may soon need to be repackaged.

Since 1979 managerial reformers have achieved many things, but many of these have been the obvious, easy targets. There are fewer of these left. It will be much harder now to show easily identifiable and tangible paybacks. As every management consultant knows, the rewards from better information systems can be vast, but they are usually unmeasurable; benefits can rarely be quantified in money terms. The emphasis in central government is moving to difficult questions of measuring performance and delegating authority and control over resources. Both issues raise unique problems in each department, since programmes, outputs and their measurability differ so widely.

A ten-year period of consistent pressure for managerial change in the public sector is unprecedented in British politics. It has been clear that the Prime Minister herself has sponsored and driven many of the initiatives. This has undoubtedly contributed to their success. But irrespective of the present administration, there is no question that many of the managerial changes will take permanent root; most have become politically neutral; some, like the major information systems projects, have absorbed major commitments of resources, which it would be absurd to write off. Managerially, there is no real alternative.

Chapter 1

Central government

It is now six years since Lord Rayner began his programme of value for money scrutinies in central government and four years since the Prime Minister launched the Financial Management Initiative. Consideration of the need for management skills and the importance of value for money are now much more a part of the way in which issues are handled in central government but there is still a long way to go before expertise in these areas can be considered of equal significance to policy advice—the traditional responsibility of the senior civil servant.

That the significant progress of the last few years has been achieved at all has been due to a combination of three factors. First, downward pressure on resources, particularly manpower, has created the need for new approaches. Secondly, a series of initiatives and programmes with strong political backing has demonstrated the scope and potential for change through practical example. Thirdly, changes in information technology and its use have offered new opportunities, leading in some large departments to wholesale reappraisal of how service delivery is organised and managed.

The key initiatives have been:

- the Financial Management Initiative (FMI), which was launched by the Prime Minister in 1982, and involved the development of management processes and planning and information systems within departments;
- the continuing programme of value for money scrutinies and reviews carried out under the aegis of the Efficiency Unit;
- systematic reviews of central services and resources such as purchasing, accommodation and central support services;

● increased concentration on personnel and training issues such as performance pay and management development.

Financial Management Initiative

The FMI is the umbrella under which all the management developments come—it provides the basic philosophy for the new approach.

The concept of the FMI is that the best way to achieve efficient and effective use of resources is to ensure that managers are clear about their objectives and have control over the necessary resources. Certain key factors flow from this basic tenet:

● that departments are clear about their overall objectives and priorities;
● that responsibilities are well-defined for individuals and for the organisation as a whole;
● that responsibility is matched by accountability;
● that individuals possess the necessary skills, incentives and information to allow them to manage their part of the organisation effectively.

Chapters 3 and 4 of the Peat Marwick book *Financial Management in the Public Sector* charted the early progress of the FMI and the impact these new approaches to management were starting to have on local office managers. Since then, the overall picture has changed little. The story is still very much one of departments making steady progress in establishing information systems, trying to acquire the relevant basic financial skills, feeling their way towards some rudimentary output and performance measures and deciding on the best approach to reorganising departmental structures and responsibilities. *Progress in Financial Management in Government Departments* (Cmnd 9297), published in July 1984, is the latest detailed account of achievement in these various areas, and subsequent published information has tended to cast light on only small parts of the FMI. Nevertheless, some four years on from the launch, the debate continues to move forward and FMI remains a major issue in central government.

One of the more important developments has been the report to the Prime Minister by the Efficiency Unit on *Consultancy, Inspection and Review Services in Government Departments* (the CIRC report). The report and its accompanying glossy handout *Helping Managers Manage* addressed the role of central services (staff inspection, management services, operations research, etc) in the context of devolved management responsibility under FMI. The conclusion of the report was that divisions performing these functions should no longer be regarded as central controllers but as service divisions which would, in future, provide help and assistance to line managers.

Line managers would control their activities through a budget which would define the resources available to them and the outputs expected of them. In addition, the report concluded that there was still a need for central support but this should not be provided via a series of specialist divisions but through a single multi-disciplinary top management support unit. This top management support unit would have an immediate key responsibility for handling the difficult period of change to budget based controls.

The twin conclusions of the report gave an important boost to the FMI approach to management and provided a further nudge to help departments in their move from highly centralised to delegated approaches to resource management and control. All departments were required to review their central services and produce proposals for change by mid-1985. This process was co-ordinated by the joint management unit (JMU) but no report of its activities has yet been published.

Departments will no doubt watch with interest to see how far the changing role between central services and line managers within departments is reflected in their relationships with central departments, in particular the Treasury. A key development here is the multi-departmental review of budgetary control systems led by Tony Wilson, the Head of the Government Accountancy Service.

The Wilson review is important for two reasons. First, before the Treasury is likely to be wholly convinced of the argument for loosening its grip on departments' affairs as a way of improving overall financial control, it will wish to be certain that strong and vigorous budgetary control systems are being developed in departments. This review provides the opportunity for the Treasury to satisfy itself that this is so. Secondly, although the FMI has concentrated a lot of thought and effort on what new forms of delegated financial control will mean for the centre, there has been much less concern with what line managers must do to be able to operate effectively in the changed environment. This again should be a key output from the review.

In addition the Wilson review is the first explicit appraisal of the discontinuity that exists between the new approaches to financial management in departments and the traditional forms of government accounting and control which have been retained at the centre such as:

- controls over manpower numbers and running costs;
- cash flow accounting;
- annuality;
- capital expenditure not handled differently from revenue;
- the treatment of receipts in isolation from associated expenditure.

A further issue which will be explored in the Wilson review is how effective departments' top management (i.e. MINIS type) systems are in setting a framework for line management budgets. The development of top management systems was a major priority for departments in their initial response to the FMI. The main aims of these systems were:

- to gather together in one place details of the objectives of the main 'businesses' of a department together with details of resources consumed by them;
- to provide information on what the 'businesses' achieved in the previous planning period and on the resources consumed by them.

Top management systems were developed primarily as a means of informing senior management, including ministers, about what was happening in the department. Once this initial aim had been achieved it was anticipated that the systems would develop into planning systems which would allow the top management of a department to set out aims, objectives and targets for the coming year(s), make decisions about resource allocation between competing schemes and review performance in a systematic way. Some departments are already reviewing their top management systems in an effort to make them strong and constructive forces. These systems are still evolving, and are difficult to design for a number of reasons:

- aims, objectives and especially targets are difficult to define for many programmes;
- the systems can easily produce too much paper and not enough information. They are, in effect, victims of the pre-FMI management style where information passes up the management line without filtration or summarisation by successive levels of management;
- departmental 'top management' is primarily concerned with policy

advice and not with management advice per se. There is still a long way to go in defining the relative management roles of ministers, permanent secretaries and deputy secretaries;

● top management reviews need to be linked into the public expenditure and supply estimates planning systems and indeed into the preparation of line management budgets within the department.

The application of the FMI to policy work is a particularly significant step since it recognises the link between programme and administrative expenditure and the need to ensure that new policy proposals have clear statements of objectives, targets, performance measures and resource costs. Management of policy programme expenditure was firmly on the FMI agenda from the outset (it is specifically included in paragraph 28 of the 1982 White Paper) but it was initially not high on anyone's list of priorities. It is not hard to see why—it was simply far too difficult to start thinking about managing policy, and people turned first to running costs and resource management, which could be more readily comprehended. Subsequently, however, attention has focused on policy work.

One of the Financial Management Unit's final reports, published in mid-1985, was on policy work in the FMI. This concluded that valuable progress is being made and good practice established in assessing the performance of programmes, but there is scope for very considerable further improvement. It found what reviewers usually find—that policy aims are often not expressed with great clarity. It contains recommendations on three main topics—responsibilities for performance assessment, the approach to performance assessment and what it calls enabling mechanisms. (Effectively, a requirement that policy reviews and initiatives should result in clear statements of how performance is to be assessed.) This area of work is being taken very seriously at present and is being pushed forward with the help of the Joint Management Unit. Policy and programmes are very often not capable of simple measurement. They can be approached through judgemental or subjective assessment of performance. But it is very much harder to convince people of the value of judgemental or subjective assessment (possibly by their peers or customers) than it is to persuade them to allow numbers to be collected.

Despite the fact that there is still a long way to go in practical implementation of the FMI, the advantages of the approach are sufficiently clear for decisions to have been taken to extend the principles of FMI to all non-departmental public bodies.

Efficiency Unit

The early work of the Efficiency Unit was described in detail in Chapter 2 of the Peat Marwick publication *Financial Management in the Public Sector*.

It is clear, however, that since Sir Robin Ibbs took over the role of Prime Minister's Adviser on Efficiency the focus of the unit has been changing. The cornerstone of its work remains the scrutiny programme, though the types of topics which are now subjected to scrutiny and the way in which they are identified have changed significantly. The scrutiny process in the Rayner era has been caricatured as an external ad hoc mechanism designed to pick off specific targets and thus demonstrate to disbelieving and uninterested officials and enthusiastic but ignorant ministers that the central government machine was vastly overweight and could be easily slimmed down if people would only attack the problem in the right way. If that was so, scrutinies offered only a short term and partial prescription which ultimately would need to be replaced by continuous and effective day-to-day management. But in reality the scrutiny programme was one part of Rayner's lasting reforms programme, which conspicuously embraced the FMI.

Sir Robin Ibbs has sought to bring the two strands more closely together by emphasising the usefulness of the scrutiny process in the context of good management within the department. He has done this by pressing departments to:

● set annual value for money targets;

● identify areas where significant improvements in value for money are required;

● use scrutinies to show how value for money improvements can be made.

The emphasis of the Efficiency Unit's work has shifted, therefore, from specific efficiency studies, with their staff and cost reduction connotations, to value for money and the wider concern for service effectiveness.

More importantly, the responsibility for defining and using the scrutiny technique has been placed fairly and squarely on ministers and top managers within departments as a means of achieving specific and logically defined targets. The scrutiny process with its value for money emphasis is being more explicitly integrated with the FMI concepts of accountability and responsibility at the apex of departments.

The whole process relies heavily on the successful operation of top management systems as planning systems, which can identify departmental priorities and set real targets for achievement. It has already been seen, however, that there are real problems here in practice. The benefit of the Ibbs approach is that it highlights the weaknesses of the departmental system in this area and also ensures that departments continue to apply their minds to the knotty problem of output and performance measurement.

Implementation of the results of scrutinies was examined in the report *Making things happen* published in Autumn 1985. This drew attention to the discrepancy between savings identified and achieved (£600m a year compared with £300m a year) and highlighted the need for greater emphasis on implementation, which it was considered should be led by permanent secretaries. As a result the scrutiny process and definition of responsibilities for its performance have been sharpened up.

Like the FMI, the scrutiny technique is also being applied across a much wider area than before. It is now used in the National Health Service and supported the Jarratt review of the Universities; it has addressed organisational problems such as those involved in the CIRC report and has also been applied in programme areas such as BBC External Services and the Urban Programme.

The scrutiny technique formed an element of the series of important multi-departmental reviews which have looked at key functions and resources. Recently these have included budgeting, government purchasing and property management. These areas consume vast amounts of resource—for example, each year departments buy goods and services worth £7,500m, excluding military spending. The purchasing review estimated that over £400m a year could be saved by streamlining purchasing arrangements through better planning of purchasing, closer liaison between purchaser and supplier and ensuring that specifications are better tuned to what the market can provide. Some of these multi-departmental reviews have been co-ordinated not by the Efficiency Unit but by the central departments (MPO and Treasury).

Personnel and training

Whilst much progress has been made on the development of top management systems, information systems and budgetary control systems, there has been less evidence of success in dealing with the underlying personnel issues which need to be addressed if FMI is to be successful.

The most significant of the issues addressed recently has been the introduction of a three-year trial for performance-related pay. The small amounts of money involved and the limited number of grades eligible for merit awards has meant that the scheme has been greeted with scepticism in many quarters. A more crucial issue, however, is how far the performance-related pay scheme can be integrated with the ideas of accountability and responsibility. The utility of the scheme from the government's viewpoint must stand or fall on this question.

The Management and Personnel Office has also turned its attention to promotion blockages at the top of the career structure and the need for improving the quality, flow and prospects of managers at lower levels. Attempts are being made to unblock the system through early retirement schemes, reviewing grade structures and increased emphasis on a policy of regular individual management development. Particular difficulties are involved in recruiting good quality professionals such as lawyers, accountants and computer staff. This is partly a pay problem but it also reflects perceptions of poor prospects and of a failure to use professional skills in general management roles.

Conclusions

In general, the trends described above are towards a much more managerial approach in government, which is seeking to learn from (and where appropriate, emulate) some of the culture, attitudes and values of the private sector. This does not mean that the Civil Service is going to be managed exactly like Marks and Spencer but it is evolving a greater commonality of approach with the understanding of this and other parts of the public sector. In due course this may lead to a greater interchange of people between sectors, which will help to reinforce these changes— although at present there remain a number of major impediments to any real mobility.

It is difficult to summarise progress in the FMI and in other managerial changes. Much has been achieved but there is still some way to go. Yet the consensus view of civil servants and others seems to be that the changes in management styles introduced over the last six or seven years are likely to be long lasting. Commitment to the main principles is not a question of party politics, and a change of administration would not have a fundamental impact on the FMI. The momentum is such that pushing through the FMI is now seen as a question of internal management rather than political initiative. All parties would accept the broad principles of the FMI. (Witness for example, the Treasury and Civil Service Committee, which has consistently shown an all-party consensus.) Any government—and especially one which wanted to expand expenditure or raise service levels—would find the FMI helpful in getting the best possible value from limited resources.

Nevertheless, there is a great deal more to achieve and significant difficulties remain—of attitudes, shortages of skills, the misconception that the FMI is about reducing spending, and a hiatus in the whole area of policy and programme management. Continuing implementation will demand significant resources both from within the service and from outside.

Chapter 2

Local authorities

There are over 500 local authorities in England, Scotland and Wales employing about 2,000,000 staff. Local authorities are central to our democratic process and pride themselves on their independence and ability to be responsive to local needs. They are also complex organisations. This chapter focuses on current key issues, dwelling on the framework within which local authorities now operate. These issues are grouped under the headings of finance, efficiency measures, local/central relationships and other developments.

Finance

Financial issues such as the scale of local authority expenditure, the level of government grant, and amendments to the capital control and the rating systems have recently dominated the policy process and have been at the nub of the debate about the relationship between central and local government.

The government's plan for local authority expenditure (Autumn 1985 statement—1986/87 figures) for England, Scotland and Wales is around £26bn per annum, with a total public spending figure of about £140bn. These figures do not necessarily reflect local authorities' practices. The divergence of view is best illustrated by reference to the figures used within the rate support grant negotiations. During the 1985/86 negotiations, it was forecast that local authorities could be spending well in excess of £2,000m per annum more than the sum allowed for in the public expenditure programme for 1986/87. This division between White Paper plans and local authority practice opens up the whole debate about the reasonableness of any grant settlement in any year. Central government compares the settlement with planned figures, whilst local authorities compare it with current levels of expenditure. This can lead to claims of a reasonable settlement figure from one side simultaneously with the contrary view from the other that settlement figures will demand significant reductions in expenditure levels.

In addition to this divergence of view as to the appropriate level of expenditure, local authority finances have been complicated further by changes in central financial support. Adjustments to the basic grants mechanism, and (until 1985/86) special penalty mechanisms have been intended to deter local authorities from exceeding central government targets and have had the effect of shifting the burden onto local ratepayers. In 1985/86 the impact of the penalty mechanisms was increased dramatically. For example, in 1984/85, where expenditure exceeded target by a little over 2%, an authority attracted accumulative penalties at a rate of 14p in the £, but this was raised to 24p in the £ for 1985/86.

It is clear that the grant system is designed to encourage local authorities to think very carefully about spending above levels deemed to be appropriate by central government. It is not unusual for the marginal pound of expenditure to cost the ratepayer £3, when the effect of all the grant mechanisms is taken into account.

A further key issue concerning local authority revenue finance is rate-capping. Indeed 1984 is likely to be remembered for the Rates Act, which gave the Secretary of State power to define an Authority's upper rate limit 'if it appears to him that expenditure is likely to be excessive having regard to general economic conditions'. In 1985/86, 18 local authorities were rate-capped. This led to much posturing and, in certain cases, litigation, after which some authorities eventually levied legal rates, whilst others continued with a policy of non-co-operation and refused to levy a legal rate until well into the 1985/86 financial year. Although not rate-capped, Liverpool City Council in 1985/86, found itself the vanguard authority in dispute with the government over the levying of a legal rate and the level of central financial support to the authority.

Nottinghamshire County Council and Bradford District Council challenged the fundamental workings of the grants system by bringing a court action. The initial ruling was in favour of the local authorities and the Court of Appeal ruled, in October 1985, that the spending targets set

17

by the Secretary of State for the Environment were unlawful; these judgements were subsequently overturned by the House of Lords.

The battle over the rate levels has thrown the spotlight once again on to the rating system, and the possible alternative ways of raising funds to finance local authorities' expenditure. The government has set up an internal enquiry into local government finance and contenders for new revenue raising measures include a per capita tax (domestic ratepayers), a national rate for business or a tax linked to capital values.

Slightly different issues have arisen in connection with central government's attempts to control local authorities' capital expenditure. Here, the problem has been how to treat capital receipts, for example, from the sales of council houses. In the initial years of the present capital system, the whole of capital receipts were available to local authorities, and could be used, for example, to top-up government-approved capital spending limits. The years 1984 and 1985 saw attempts to limit authorities' freedom to supplement prescribed expenditure allocations in this way. In seeking ways to circumvent potential restraints, local authorities have alighted on some original schemes. The legal aspects of these transactions are intricate, but, broadly, they are intended to ensure that advantage can be taken of the proceeds of sales of assets in the form of increased capital spending approvals. For example, some local authorities have entered into arrangements with merchant banks to make advance payments on works which will subsequently be commissioned by those banks.

The financial manoeuvring raises the topic of creative accounting, i.e. book-keeping adjustments designed to massage expenditure so as to minimise the constraints imposed through the revenue and capital control mechanisms. Actual expenditure is not affected and therefore an element of artificiality is introduced into national figures and renders comparisons over time unreliable. Measures include capitalising revenue expenditure, altering debt repayment schedules, selling off assets to generate capital receipts, the extensive use of reserves and creating and closing down funds. It is a sad irony that so much talent and creative flair has been diverted to this activity.

Efficiency measures

Local authorities have been active in the field of efficiency studies for many years, well before Rayner studies and NHS cost-improvement programmes. But the work of individual authorities has not been publicised and, in the public perception, efficiency measures in local authorities are associated with the Audit Commission's 'Three Es' studies.

The creation of the Commission was viewed with some trepidation in local government circles, many fearing that in practice it would be no more than another arm of central government charged with castigating local authorities. These fears have proved groundless and the Commission has gained a reputation for its independence. The activities of the Commission that have generated the most interest and comment are its special studies. A general theme of these studies is that there is much to praise within local government, whilst significant improvements could be made if there was widespread adoption of the good practices of the more efficient and effective authorities. For example, if all authorities were to secure the prices obtained by the more successful operations it is suggested that as much as £200m per annum could be saved. A study of further education showed that substantial improvements could be made in academic staffing, cost recovery, control of non-teaching costs and marketing.

Two studies into the block grant system and capital control system have been particularly welcomed by local government, no doubt largely because they tend to support the arguments put forward by local authorities upon these matters over the years. The major criticism made of these systems is that neither assists the promotion of efficiency and effectiveness, and that the costs thereby incurred by local authorities are higher. For example, the Commission argues that councils have had to collect more from ratepayers than might otherwise have been the case as a direct consequence of the uncertainties within the grant system. The Commission has also stated that capital controls preclude the rational consideration of priorities and full appraisal of potential investments. It will be interesting to observe whether either report makes any impact upon the way central government operates in future.

Local/central relationships

Local/central relationships are clearly at a low ebb. The main issue, which underlies all the debates referred to above, is constitutional—that is, the right of a local authority to manage its own affairs and provide the services it considers necessary. The most obvious barometer of the strained relationship between local and central government is litigation.

The years 1984 and 1985 have seen much local/central litigation, perhaps fired by the GLC and London borough cases of a few years earlier. Authorities display a new readiness to take the Secretary of State (and indeed each other) to court. The GLC, for example, challenged the sum it was required to pay to the new body, London Regional Transport; Derbyshire County Council challenged the reasonableness of their spending targets; the Secretary of State was subject to litigation over his unwillingness to disclose the underlying detail of his rate-capping calculations; and, catching the prevailing mood, a member of the public took Hackney Council to Court with a view to obtaining an order instructing that authority to make a rate. Added to the Nottinghamshire County Council and Bradford District Council case referred to earlier, these are but a few examples of the trend towards litigation.

A fundamental reappraisal and redefinition of the respective, and complementary, roles of local and central government is needed to break out of the current sequence of ad hoc responses to perceived problems, by central government, followed by challenges to these measures by local authorities. The teachers' dispute has thrown up all the ambiguities of responsibility, identity of paymaster and of policy determination characteristic of the local/central divide.

The reorganisation of metropolitan government

Following the reorganisation of local government in the metropolitan areas, responsibilities for the services provided by the GLC and the Metropolitan County Councils will be assigned to other bodies. Joint Authorities will be created for the fire service and, outside London, for police and public transport. These Joint Authorities have had detailed controls over their finance and manpower imposed on them which are unprecedented in local government. Central government will take to itself Green Belt issues, for example, and a Planning Commission will deal with strategic planning for the London area. The bulk of the services, numerically, but not in terms of expenditure, pass to London boroughs or metropolitan districts, including waste disposal, trading standards, concessionary fares, safety at sports grounds, assistance to industry and support for voluntary bodies. There are also residuary bodies charged with winding up the affairs of the councils and administering those matters which do not readily lend themselves to transfer to a successor body in the short term, e.g. debt management, superannuation funds, unassigned legal rights and liabilities, property disposal and central computing. Peat Marwick undertook, for the Department of the Environment, a comprehensive study of the practical tasks facing the Residuary Bodies, at the time the Local Government Act 1985 became law.

The Widdicombe enquiry

In the course of recent controversies in local government, two issues affecting the political activities of the council and its members have come to a head. One is the use of public funds for overtly party political publicity campaigns—the other is the political activity of local authority employees, who, currently, are barred only from serving as members on their own employing authority. These, and other aspects of the politicising of the administrative environment of local government, are being studied by the Widdicombe enquiry.

Competitive tendering

Local authorities, having coped with the direct labour legislation, are now faced with further proposals for competition in some services. Although the timescale for legislation has yet to be determined, central government is known to be considering extending the DLO principles to other services, such as refuse collection, street cleansing, maintenance of parks and sports grounds and maintenance of vehicles. The competitive philosophy has already been introduced into municipal transport undertakings with the passing of the Transport Act 1985, requiring local authorities to set up, at arms-length, companies to run their transport undertakings. Peat Marwick has assisted various authorities to set up companies and to produce business plans, and has advised upon information systems and management structures and processes.

Consultation with business ratepayers

For the 1985/86 budget process local authorities had to take account of the Rates Act 1984 and its requirement to consult with business interests. Various notes of guidance were issued and duties placed upon authorities to disclose certain information (such as manpower statistics) to the consultees. The legislation became effective a little too late to make much impact upon the 1985/86 process, but in 1986/87 might be more meaningful.

Organisation reviews and job evaluation

The far-reaching structural reviews of the 1960s are generally not being replicated in the 1980s but it is interesting to note the number of authorities which are changing their management structures. Chief executives are still a vulnerable breed. Information technology has sired information officers. There has been a tendency to merge land, property-building and engineering functions, whilst economic development initiatives have led to new divisions or departments, as has some authorities' concern with the whole question of equal opportunities.

Job evaluation exercises, particularly for the senior management of local authorities, are also more common. New remuneration packages and contractual terms are being introduced and there is evidence of a move away from standardised conditions of service.

Conclusions

Drawing general conclusions about the impact of these issues on local authority management is not easy but a number of interrelated factors can be discerned which will continue to affect management in local authorities:

- continuing conflicts, especially in local/central relationships;
- uncertainty: for example, in the level of government grant;
- significant change: for example, arising from Metropolitan reorganisation or from new technology;

- tension: for example, arising from differing perceptions of member/officer relationships;
- restriction of role: for example, the limiting of local authority direct control through the Transport Act 1985;
- pressures for uniformity, as both levels of service and methods of delivery are increasingly challenged.

The year 1986/87 will be a true test of managerial competence and of the corporate spirit of local government—even without the continual demand for more and better services at a reduced total cost! The range and magnitude of the problems facing local government are awesome.

Chapter 3

Efficiency reviews of the nationalised industries

The 1945 Labour government intended to leave the running of the nationalised industries to their boards, who were given only loosely defined statutory objectives. Concern about the industries' performance led to successive White Papers laying down more detailed guidelines and financial and economic objectives. However, there remained the problem of checking that the industries were actually following the guidelines and operating efficiently.

The 1978 White Paper, *The Nationalised Industries* (Cmnd 7131) recognised that the arm's length approach was no longer appropriate. Arrangements for efficiency review took concrete form with the Competition Act 1980, which gave the Secretary of State for Trade (now Trade and Industry) powers to order efficiency reviews by the Monopolies and Mergers Commission. In addition, a number of efficiency reviews by management consultants have been commissioned*.

The Competition Act 1980

Section 11 of the Competition Act 1980 applies to nationalised industries, water authorities, bus undertakings and agricultural marketing boards. It empowers the Trade Secretary to refer to the Commission any question relative to:

● efficiency and costs;

*See *Investigating Public Industries: how has the Monopolies and Mergers Commission performed?* by Barrie Collins & Bob Wharton, Public Money, September 1984 and *Efficiency Studies of Nationalised Industries* by Bob Wharton, Public Money, September 1985.

- the service provided;
- possible abuse of monopoly.

The Commission is usually asked in the terms of reference to report on whether the industry is pursuing a course of conduct which operated against the public interest. If the Commission finds that this is so, the Act gives the sponsoring Minister power to order the industry to produce a plan to remedy the problem.

Section 11 references now account for over 60% of the Commission's total workload. The Commission is allowed up to nine months to present its report to the Secretary for Trade and Industry (though further time may then elapse before publication). Early studies had wide scope, and the Commission apparently found it difficult to complete them within the deadline. More recently, the Commission has undertaken more studies per year, but each review has usually focused on a narrower range of activities. Table 1 summarises the studies undertaken.

The terms of reference of studies typically ask the Commission to investigate whether the industry could improve its efficiency and thus reduce its costs without affecting the standard of service to consumers. Quality of service is therefore usually within the Commission's terms of reference. There may also be a list of particular items to which the Commission is asked to give attention. Investment appraisal, budgetary control, maintenance management and manpower productivity have been items frequently specified, though the Commission does not restrict itself to the items listed.

The Monopolies Commission approach

The Commission has wide powers of access to persons and papers. Its reviews involve in-depth investigation of documents and interview programmes conducted by teams of staff members. These lead up to hearings, at which Commission members take evidence from industry management and third parties in a courtroom atmosphere. The formality of these procedures can make them something of an ordeal for the participants.

The Commission concentrates on policies, systems and procedures, rather than looking for detailed economies or second, guessing minor decisions. Its work results in voluminous reports which give detailed evidence to support the conclusions. They include valuable information that would not otherwise be publicly available (and which might not have been available to the sponsoring department). One drawback is that it is often difficult to isolate key findings and recommendations from the descriptive material.

The Commission has evolved a set of 'paradigms'—ideals of good practice—with which it compares actual practice. The paradigms are based on accepted good professional practice and on the guidelines set out in White Papers. Some of the more important paradigms are considered below.

Management structure

The Commission has encouraged part-time board members to play an active part in pressing for greater efficiency. Part-time members should make up the Audit Committee of the board and receive reports from a central efficiency unit.

Financial planning and control

The Commission expects the framework for financial planning to be set by the industry's corporate plan, which should include an evaluation of the options available. The budget should be consistent with the first year of the corporate plan. The Commission has criticised the 'incremental approach' to budgeting; it prefers to see financial budgets related to physical objectives, and to see unit cost reduction targets incorporated in the budget setting process. The management information system should support the planning and budgeting process. Actual results should be reported regularly against budget, and corrective action should be taken where significant variances emerge. The Commission favours keeping the lowest level of budget responsibility well down the management hierarchy. For example, London Transport reported bus maintenance costs at district level only; the Commission believed that each garage should be a cost centre, and that a clearer role should be given to the Garage Engineering Manager.

Investment appraisal

The existence of well-established standards of good practice (White Papers, Treasury guidelines, the writings of accountants and economists in the private and public sectors) may explain why the Commission has devoted considerable attention to investment appraisal. The large size of the industries' programmes may also be a factor. Surprisingly, given that the guidelines are so well-established, the Commission has found much to criticise.

The main problems lie not in the mechanics of applying discounted cash-flow techniques, but in selecting options for appraisal, forecasting costs and revenues, exploring the sensitivity of results and determining priorities. For example, the Commission's analysis of projects completed by the National Coal Board showed that some areas had been consistently optimistic in forecasting the productivity of proposed projects and underestimated the time taken to complete them. Projects had tended to develop a momentum with expenditure being committed in advance of the project being approved. Projects were not reconsidered once approval was given, even though there were cases where it was apparent at an early stage that all was not going to plan. The Board had not considered all relevant alternatives. In particular, it considered that closure of a pit with workable reserves was not a realistic option. There was no clear procedure for setting investment priorities. As a result of these factors, more than a third of the Board's investment had been in pits that were of doubtful future profitability.

Use of manpower
In production operations the Commission expects to find measured time standards providing the basis for incentive schemes and for production planning. Time actually spent on jobs should be recorded, to allow accurate job costing and provide information for manpower planning.

The public interest
The concept of the public interest has never been tightly defined by the legislation and the Commission is left to make a judgement on the facts of the case. It has found three cases of conduct contrary to the public interest:

- the CEGB, whose investment appraisals were held to be *seriously defective and liable to mislead*;
- the Severn Trent Water Authority, whose headquarters had exercised

inadequate control over divisions and therefore could not effectively secure cost savings;

- Caledonian MacBrayne, which had given discriminatory discounts to a road haulage subsidiary.

Follow-up

Statutory provision for follow-up exists only where the Commission has made a public interest finding. In practice a standard follow-up procedure has evolved, regardless of the public interest factor. The industry normally makes a response to the Commission's report within about three months, and is supposed to make a further report on progress in implementation a year later.

Responses vary in tone from highly defensive to constructive. Where the Commission's recommendations are cautious or 'coded' (which they often are) the industry can easily ignore the nuances.

In many cases it appears that the Commission's reports strengthen the hand of the sponsoring ministry in pressing the industry to improve efficiency. Where the Commission touches on major policy issues, follow-up becomes less clear. Criticism of the CEGB's investment appraisals cast embarrassing doubt on nuclear power policy on the eve of the Sizewell inquiry. It was almost two years before the Energy Secretary announced that he had received the CEGB's response and that he was satisfied with the improvements made to appraisal procedures.

The Commission's reports generally receive little publicity, and have perhaps less influence than they deserve. There is, for example, little evidence that MPs have studied them. In part this may be because the reports are not easy reading for busy people. Industry responses are 'published' by being placed in the House of Commons Library, where they are readily available only to MPs.

Studies by management consultants

In addition to the work of the Monopolies Commission, a number of similar studies have been undertaken by management consultants. Table

2 lists those which have been published. A much larger number of unpublished studies have been carried out by consultants.

Follow-up of these reports appears to have been similar to follow-up of Monopolies Commission work. The study of the BBC, of which only a summary has been published, received widespread public attention, as did that of British Airways (which was not formally published); but the others received little notice.

Management consultants are, of course, frequently used by the Commission to assist it in the conduct of studies which require substantial resources in a short timescale.

Some issues

The Monopolies Commission has already survived one challenge to its efficiency review role. Mr. Norman St. John-Stevas's Parliamentary Control of Expenditure (Reform) Bill would have replaced the Commission by the Comptroller and Auditor General. This provision had been dropped by the time the Bill emerged as the National Audit Act 1983.

The Monopolies Commission has begun to include in its reports a more readable general assessment which may sharpen their impact. It could do more by:

● making recommendations on what performance indicators the industries should be reporting in their annual accounts. This would make it easier for outsiders to judge what progress was being made;

● being more explicit about its paradigms. These could be published as statements of good practice for public sector management. At present they have to be deduced from the reports themselves;

● including in its annual report (published as part of the annual report of the Office of Fair Trading) a summary of MMC reports, the responses made by the industries and any follow-up.

Table 1

Monopolies Commission studies under the Competition Act 1980

Industry	Date of publication
British Rail (London and South East commuter services)	1980
Severn Trent Water Authority	1981
CEGB	1981
Anglian Water Authority and North West Water Authority (sewerage function)	1982
Bristol Omnibus Co, Trent Motor Traction, Cardiff City Transport and West Midlands PTE (bus operations)	1982
National Coal Board (Production and supply of coal)	1983
Yorkshire Electricity Board	1983
Caledonian Macbrayne Ltd. (Shipping services)	1983
Civil Aviation Authority (air traffic control services)	1983
London Transport Executive (maintenance of buses)	1984
South Wales Electricity Board	1984
The Post Office Letter Post Service (letter service in Glasgow, Belfast, Cardiff and London)	1984
Yorkshire Water Authority	1984
The Revenue Collection Systems of four Area Electricity Boards	1985

Industry	Date of publication
British Rail (property management)	1985
North of Scotland Hydro-Electric Board	1985
British Airports Authority (commercial activities)	1985
Southern Water Authority	due 1986
South of Scotland Electricity Board	due 1986
British Steel Corporation	due 1986
Post Office (procurement activities)	due 1986

Table 2

Published efficiency studies of nationalised industries conducted by consultants

Industry	Study by	Date of publication
South of Scotland Electricity Board	Coopers & Lybrand Associates	1982
UK Atomic Energy Authority	Peat, Marwick, Mitchell & Co.	1982
British Gas Corporation	Deloitte, Haskins & Sells	1983
North of Scotland Hydro-Electric Board	Arthur Young McClelland Moores & Co.	1983
Northern Ireland Electricity Service	Beecom Management Consultants Ltd. with Armitage Norton Consultants and Ewbank & Partners Ltd.	1983
BBC	Peat, Marwick, Mitchell & Co.	1985

Chapter 4

Universities

The publication in Spring 1985 of both the Green Paper on higher education (Cmnd 9524) and the Jarratt Report on University management and efficiency *(Report of the Steering Committee for Efficiency Studies in Universities*, CVCP, March 1985) has focused attention on a sector that poses particular difficulties for attempts to assess value for money. Although they are private bodies, the universities are largely dependent upon the government for support—to the extent in 1982-83 of about £1,250m in direct recurrent grant from the University Grants Committee (UGC) and about £750m in local authority support of fees and maintenance (which in turn attracts central government support). It is not surprising therefore that, following similar trends in central government and the NHS, the management and efficiency of the universities has come increasingly under scrutiny.

The sensitivity and difficulty of this area is highlighted by the intensity of the debate on a range of issues related to the cost and value of higher education. These include:

- student loans and parental contributions;
- overseas student fees;
- tenure for academic staff;
- the relevance of university degrees to the economic needs of the nation;
- the relative cost and value of university and polytechnic courses;
- the desirability and scope for rationalising the existing pattern of universities and departments.

The Jarratt report drew attention to the need for a stable planning horizon and recommended that the universities should seriously examine their ability to take difficult planning and resource allocation decisions (with the presumption of difficult financial times ahead). The Green Paper has emphasised the need for these changes with projections of falling student numbers and falling real levels of government support. In this chapter we review the main issues at the centre of this debate.

Recent trends—expansion then cuts

There are 47 universities in Britain. They employ about 30,000 academic staff. There were just under 300,000 students at universities in 1982/83 of whom 250,000 were undergraduates and 27,000 were from overseas. There were also about 260,000 students at polytechnics and other colleges of advanced education—generally referred to as 'the public sector' in higher education. Since the war there has been a general trend to expansion of the university sector. This was particularly marked in the 1960s when many new universities were founded and existing ones expanded. Much new university building was carried out in this period—a fact that has implications for required levels of maintenance and renewal today.

This expansion was abruptly halted in 1981 when the University Grants Committee announced cuts in recurrent grants to universities that ranged from 6% to 44% with an average of 17%. Even for universities that experienced the more modest reductions these July 1981 cuts were a traumatic experience. An average of 70% of university expenditure is on pay, and academic staff generally have (or are believed to have) tenure—i.e. appointment for life. The universities' room for manoeuvre was therefore very restricted. Most cut back on items that could be deferred (like building maintenance) and large numbers of staff retired early, leaving unplanned gaps in the teaching and research strength. For the most severely affected university, Salford, it was necessary to rethink its whole role, objectives and sources of support. This process resulted in changes aimed at attracting a much greater level of support and involvement from industry—an outcome that seems favoured by the government in its Green Paper.

Although subsequent windfall grants from the UGC alleviated their severity, the 1981 cuts imposed strains throughout the university system because it was ill-adapted to deal with them. Universities had developed systems of self-government based on the need to promote scholarship—excellence in teaching and research. These systems could cope quite well with periods of expansion, but were less suited to taking hard decisions about allocating diminishing resources, or to exploiting the commercial and income-generating potential of their institutions. The reconciliation of these relatively recent management imperatives with their traditional scholarship role is probably the major challenge facing the universities today. It emerged as the central theme of the Jarratt report which represents an amalgam of views and experience from six different universities which participated in the study and six firms of consultants who assisted them.

The university culture—participation and democracy

The challenge facing the universities is of course similar to that facing all public sector bodies. What makes the issue particularly acute for the universities is their unique and highly participative system of government. A university might be characterised as a community of scholars, each eminent in his or her own field, but none of whom would normally presume to pass judgement over colleagues in other fields. These scholars come together for the convenience of shared facilities and services and for the intellectual vigour and stimulation that comes from cross-fertilisation of ideas. They relate to each other and to their students as individuals and in a generally non-hierarchical fashion. The consequence is that the attitudes and disciplines of commercial management have generally been felt to be inappropriate in a university. The use of the term manager would often be regarded with suspicion by professional staff who have been appointed as independent scholars with no clear line management role.

The investigations of the Jarratt Committee encountered many manifestations of this particular culture. For example:

- most academics claimed that the objectives of their university were the promotion of excellence in teaching and research across a broad range of disciplines. It was often difficult to identify more specific objectives, or to measure progress towards them;
- the absence of a clear management hierarchy means that any decision on academic matters that has implications beyond an individual subject or course has to be taken by consensus in a body on which all senior academics are represented. This supreme academic body is the University Senate and may have well over 100 members (182 at Nottingham, for example);

- this consensus approach is very conservative. Changes in resource levels tend to be allocated to departments on a strictly pro rata basis, thereby freezing the university's pattern of departments in the status quo and making it difficult to open new areas or departments or to make decisive shifts in the balance of subjects;
- as a result of incremental cuts, effectiveness may be reduced in many areas and small departments may be weakened to the point of non-viability. The UGC has recently made clear its concern about the problem of small departments;
- initiatives to generate external, industrial income for the university have no clear focus (unless limited to a single department). They may be seen as peripheral to the university's main objectives and therefore of low priority in competing for scarce academic resources.

University government

Most universities have a bi-cameral system of government. The Senate, already mentioned, is the supreme academic authority, usually a highly democratic and participative body but inevitably not a very efficient one. The second main body, the Council, is usually smaller with an important complement of lay members (i.e. not employed by the university). Council has responsibility for all financial matters including the ultimate approval of appointments and the maintenance of the estate (often a major consideration) and acts as the court of appeal for matters which cannot be resolved elsewhere. The lay membership of Council serves both to introduce outside experience and expertise to university government and to act as a visible reassurance that public money is used in a responsible fashion. The Council may have the power to veto or send back Senate proposals involving expenditure and is thus the superior body. Normally Senate and Council operate in different areas and conflict is avoided. It is much more difficult to avoid however when, as at present, resources are constrained and academic priorities may have to give way to broader considerations such as the maintenance of buildings.

The Council and Senate each have sub-committees dealing with particular areas of their responsibility. This committee structure can become very complex and extends down into faculty and departmental committees. The University of Nottingham, for example, has some 60 formal committees, and it has been estimated that the academic time spent attending committees there is the equivalent of nine members of academic staff working full time, with corresponding demands for administrative staff to service the committees. This is not an unusual situation—some other universities have even more complex committee structures.

Although they play an essential role, university committees are generally unwieldly formal bodies and much of the day-to-day management of a university is carried out by officers and by informal structures. The chief officer is the Vice-Chancellor (VC) who is both the principal academic officer (chairman of Senate) and the principal administrative officer (heading the administration). He or she will also be a powerful member of Council and of its major sub-committees. Books have been written about the role of the Vice-Chancellor and there are as many styles of Vice-Chancellor as there are universities. The range of responsibilities is enormous. The Vice-Chancellor has to provide the leadership without which the consensus/committee based system will not be able to create and adapt to the changes that are increasingly necessary, resolve the tensions between the Senate and Council viewpoints, command the confidence of the academics, maintain the reputation of the university (without which student demand and resources will fall) and justify to an increasingly sceptical public and government the amount of public funds devoted to universities.

The Vice-Chancellor has very limited powers since he has to work through the committee structure where he can always be out-voted. On administrative matters he can take executive action through his senior full-time officers—usually a Registrar heading an administration with several departments, sometimes a Registrar and Bursar of equal status. On academic matters he can call upon support from (usually three) Pro-Vice-Chancellors (PVCs), academics who serve for about three years as deputies to the VC in certain areas of his responsibility. The other academic officers are Deans of faculties usually elected from among the heads of department within a faculty, and heads of department. There are few clear instances of line management on the academic side, so that the VC usually has to deal direct with department heads (of whom there may be 50-100 in a large university) on any matters affecting individual departments. A key factor here is the role of Deans. Although in certain institutions the Dean may act as an intermediate level of accountable management on resource and performance issues, it is more common for this to be a largely academic role held in rotation by the relevant heads of department serving for perhaps three years each.

The Jarratt study recognised the special features of university life that influence their governing structure, but made several suggestions for changes in emphasis and practice to reflect anticipated future needs. These included:

- a stronger role for Councils and within them for younger, commercially-minded laymen;
- streamlining of committee structures and more efficient use of the staff time they consume;
- sensible use of informal structures such as informal cabinets;
- appropriate training for Vice-Chancellors and other office holders;
- greater delegation of budgets and accountability to departments;
- more emphasis on staff development including the introduction of an annual staff review procedure.

University planning

The Jarratt report identified planning and use of resources as the area where the universities have the greatest opportunity to improve their efficiency and effectiveness. The consensus/committee style of management described above gives great weight to the views of existing departments and this can mean a resistance to change. This may be tolerable in the very short term or when resources are relatively unconstrained, but if maintained during difficult times it risks leaving the university drifting and vulnerable to further pressures. It is in sharp contrast with the UGC's desire that universities should acquire a deliberate bias towards change.

Planning is difficult for universities because of the uncertain resource climate. They have suffered from stop-go swings in advice from the UGC and from very late announcement of grant—sometimes after the academic year has begun. The UGC recurrent grant mechanisms are about to undergo radical changes but are currently related to student number quotas in the three broad categories—arts, science and medicine and the university has to decide how to allocate student numbers, and the resources that go with them, between its faculties and departments. Student admissions are granted principally on the basis of 'A' level scores and so a careful juggling process is required to set the admissions standard at the point where the university will not be embarrassed (and perhaps penalised by the UGC) by taking in too many or too few students against the quota. Overseas students, who now pay what has been called 'a full economic fee', add a further complication. They are not subject to UGC quotas and so can represent a useful source of additional income. Many universities have, however, introduced internal quotas on overseas student numbers.

The general picture as observed in the Jarratt study is that responsibility for planning is often spread between several committees, that there is little or no overall planning beyond the short term, and that different types of resources are often allocated to departments by different committees so that there is no central view of the overall costs of a department. It is rare to find any formal evaluation of what is achieved with these resources or any agreement on strengths or weaknesses of the university as a basis for future action.

Jarratt's main proposals for improvement of the planning and resource allocation process are:

- a small joint committee of Senate and Council to integrate academic, physical and financial planning;
- clear arrangements subordinate to this committee for allocating the different academic resources (staff, space, equipment and services);
- budget centres made aware of their costs and given a controlled degree of freedom and incentive to optimise use of their resources;
- improved management information and performance indicators.

Value for money

The application of these proposals to university management will not be easy although the theoretical justification for them is probably broadly accepted. What difference will they make to the taxpayer or the student seeking the best value for the inevitably limited money available for higher education? How indeed can we tell if the universities do in fact offer adequate value for money and how can this value for money be improved?

These questions are difficult to answer, chiefly because it is very difficult to evaluate the output of a university despite the sincere attempts that have been made. Clearly a graduate has a market value. One recent survey suggested that in terms of initial earning potential of their graduates, polytechnics are more successful than most universities. However, one should look over a reasonable timespan (the graduate's whole career?) and graduates are not the only output: how can the value of research work, stimulus to industry, continuing education, the universities' contribution to their local communities, to national cultural life and to the image of the UK abroad be evaluated? Most of these are intangible but it is possible to envisage rather more helpful measures of the quality of teaching and research than are currently used. The indicators that universities themselves quote when they are trying to impress the UGC are usually measures of input such as average 'A' level scores of applicants, and number of research grants won rather than output.

There is a need for the universities to pay much more serious attention to the value they add to these inputs and to seek to develop performance indicators and output measures to help them monitor and improve this. It is fairly normal practice on commercial and business courses for paying students to be invited to evaluate the quality and relevance of the teaching they receive. Some university departments do this already; it could be a salutary experience for others! Peer review is a well established mechanism for assessment of research. It has been much criticised as cosy and incestuous although some of these criticisms can be answered by using outside peers. Why not apply some such assessment to the teaching, curriculum development and departmental management activities of academic staff as well? What is clear is that some form of evaluation must be attempted and the universities would surely do better to develop this for themselves than to have it imposed upon them from outside.

Staff appraisal

The staff appraisal procedure that has been recommended by the Jarratt committee should help to focus attention on the performance of academics. At present, recruitment, promotion and even movement between universities are all very constrained by cuts, as are funds for conferences and other 'rewards' for academics. It is therefore important to ensure that the most able young staff are not alienated and demotivated by a system that does not recognise or reward their efforts, while providing totally secure lifelong employment to all their colleagues irrespective of their current contribution to the university. The existence of tenure coupled with the self-governing nature of Senates can make the academic appear a highly privileged person. It will be argued that the special nature of scholarship and the element of peer review that it involves justifies this isolation from the career pressures faced by most other professions. However, the universities will need to re-examine the criteria for promotion and reward of staff and to accept the need to remove incompetent staff if they wish to continue to command public confidence in their management of public funds.

Business and income generating activities

However successful the universities are at improving their efficiency and demonstrating that they offer value for money, there will be pressures upon them to broaden the basis of their funding. There are two main reasons for doing this:

- to reduce their dependence upon the UGC and hence their dependence on shifts in government financial policy;
- to develop closer links with their local communities and with the business world as a means to broaden the perceived relevance and appeal of universities in the community.

Most universities have some sources of funding apart from the UGC, but until recently these have usually been either relatively minor or else the result of past endowments and investments. In recent years there has been an upsurge in business-related and income-generating activities at many universities. Typically these may include:

- profitable exploitation of spare capacity in facilities for academic purposes (e.g. university farms, computing services);
- development of conference business which increases the use of halls of residence and catering facilities in vacations;
- development of research and consultancy links with local industry;
- exploiting the loyalty and current income of past students.

All these activities are natural extensions of the academic aims of a university and their development might not be expected to pose any difficulties. However, despite some impressive initiatives and the example of institutions such as Salford and Cranfield, universities in general have

41

perhaps been rather slow to develop them. There are several reasons for this:

- a fear that the UGC would penalise such efforts at self-help by reducing its recurrent grant to universities which have increased their income from other sources;
- the difficulty of finding the initial investment of resources that is needed to develop income-generating activities;
- the fact that academics are in general not selected, trained or rewarded for their ability to generate income for the university and that the consensus nature of university government, coupled with the strict controls on use of public money, makes it quite difficult to offer them any incentives to do so.

The new management approach recommended by Jarratt should help the universities to develop business activities if they wish to, and to make the decisions that are needed to allocate resources and priority to potentially profitable activities. A key to this development will be the ability to recognise the different contributions that academic staff can make and to encourage and reward these appropriately.

The future

The financial pressures that have affected other parts of the public sector will have a profound impact on the universities. Demographic changes will cause the university-age population to fall markedly in the next ten years and it is clear that the 1981 reduction in government support was not simply a single year's aberration. At the same time there are serious shortages of skills in the economy and there are other largely untapped markets for the services universities have to offer. These include continuing adult education, overseas students, research, industrial co-operation, consultancy and conference business. The Green Paper refers to the possibility of closures and it cannot be assumed that the present pattern of universities and departments will automatically continue to command government support.

The UGC now has the opportunity to play a role in sharpening the objectives of the universities and in giving them encouragement and incentives to develop their own strengths and to become less dependent upon government funding. The Government has recently announced a review of the functions, structure and membership of the UGC. This is being conducted by a committee chaired by Lord Croham and may help in this shift of emphasis. If it does, the next few years should see a range of interesting developments in the university sector. It is to be hoped that the universities will rise to the challenge and that we shall see a responsive, well-managed, university system that is able to face an uncertain future with confidence while retaining the best traditions of democracy and scholarship that have rightly made UK higher education admired world-wide.

Chapter 5

The health service

The NHS is one of the largest employers in Europe, with over 800,000 staff and a budget of £16,000m per annum. Expenditure in the UK on health care in the public and private sector is 5.9% of the GDP (OECD figures) compared with 10.6% in the US, 9.7% in Sweden and 8.2% in West Germany. These figures are not particularly helpful, as the most important issue is whether value for money is obtained. However, there are difficulties in measuring outcome (as opposed to output) and quality of service.

In discussing the NHS it is important to look at the process of management and review mechanisms and the ways in which central initiatives have, or have not, stimulated improvements in high cost areas. Key among these initiatives has been the Griffiths report which has been integrated with many other central initiatives.

The Griffiths Report—recommendations and implementation

The management inquiry team led by Roy Griffiths, managing director of Sainsburys, produced one of the most significant reports on the NHS for many years. The report was short, styled in the form of a letter to the Secretary of State, and produced quickly. The impact of the report, when published in October 1983, was immediate. The recommendations included:

- the creation of an NHS supervisory board, and also a management board;
- the appointment of general managers at regional, district and unit level;

- the clarification of roles of members and officers;
- the introduction of personal accountability;
- an increase in delegation;
- improved financial management (including clinical budgeting);
- greater emphasis on personnel, planning, estate and information services.

The Secretary of State accepted the recommendations and quickly established the supervisory board, chaired by himself. The appointment of the chairman of the management board took some time, as did some other appointments, for example of the director of personnel, which was not made until October 1985.

As a result of the Griffiths report, management style has changed from that of consensus management to one much more akin to a business management model. The appointment of general managers, with considerable authority and personal accountability, has signalled the beginning of a change in attitudes and has been received with mixed feelings.

People with different backgrounds were appointed as general managers; whilst a large number of appointments were made from former regional and district administrators, there were also appointments of people with medical, nursing, finance, industry, army and other backgrounds. The appointment procedures were seen by some as unfair, and several resignations occurred over the role played by the DHSS.

Whilst many will sympathise with NHS staff who have been through the 1974, 1982 and 1984/5 reorganisations, reorganisation need not always be bad. In some industries, reorganisation occurs frequently to meet changes in environment, products and technology, or to inject increased motivation. If staff understand the need for change, and have confidence in the management of that change and in those leading the process, morale can be maintained. General managers have had a difficult task so far and this will increase as unit general managers are appointed and start to tackle direct patient care areas.

The role of the general manager

The general manager provides leadership and a central focus. It is his or her task to seek positive improvements in management, including planning, personnel, information systems and estate management. He needs to propose, agree and implement changes in management structures, initiate changes in attitude and highlight individual accountability. The general manager determines priorities with the health authority and its professional advisers. He will need to develop effective working relationships with key staff, especially consultants and general practitioners, and will need to harness the professional skills of his colleagues (and their management talents) to his own management and political skills.

He will need to analyse, with the appropriate professions, health outputs, and start to look critically at outcomes. The commissioning of proper market research to ensure that the consumer's voice is heard is important, and managers will need to be proactive in public relations. Their role is to reduce complex issues to the essentials for timely decisions, and to find opportunities, not obstacles.

Lines of accountability

The DHSS, through the supervisory and management boards, will set overall policy guidelines and will be the highest level in the accountability process.

The regions, as statutorily established corporate bodies, will translate policy guidelines on resources and care group priorities into specific objectives. They will be monitored in this by the DHSS through a range of activities, including the formal review process.

The districts, also statutorily established corporate bodies, will further refine the guidelines and act as the operational organisation for the delivery of care.

At unit level, the delivery of direct patient care will be the responsibility, ultimately, of the unit general manager. Unit general managers will be directly accountable to the district general manager, irrespective of the prior discipline of either manager. District general managers will be accountable to the district health authority for the total management performance of the district. However, there will still be direct access to the authority by certain professional staff, for example nurses, on strictly professional issues.

46

District general managers will not be accountable to regional general managers, although there will clearly be a monitoring function exercised by the RGM, and a leverage applied because of the resource allocation role of the region. Equally, regional general managers will be accountable to their own health authority, and not to the DHSS. The allocation of funds from the centre, however, will have a significant influence on the way that the RGMs operate.

Whilst there is a relatively clear picture of formal accountability and monitoring/liaison roles, the effect of fixed-term contracts is not at all clear. All general managers were appointed on three to five year fixed-term contracts and it remains to be seen how much this influences their performance, and in what way.

Key issues in the first three years

The general manager must implement revised management structures quickly and sensitively, and restore morale, especially amongst certain groups of staff, for example nurses. He must evaluate critically the range of services provided, challenging traditional practices with sensitivity. Changes which will benefit patients and potential patients will need to be made with the minimum of delay.

The general manager will need to introduce and develop management (including clinical) budgeting systems, and to ensure that they integrate financial, manpower and activity data. He must vigorously pursue all possible areas of savings, using the value for money techniques widely available. In addition, he must look at ways of improving the levels of income available to supplement central allocations. Another priority will be to progress policies of locally-based, community-orientated services for the mentally ill, the mentally handicapped and the elderly. He must aim to provide a service which is well-balanced clinically and geographically.

Information needs of general managers

No manager can be effective without timely, relevant and reliable information. It is anticipated that in the medium to longer term this will be available through management budgeting and the implementation of the Körner proposals. The work undertaken by the joint NHS/DHSS steering group, founded in 1980 and chaired by Mrs Körner, was the result of widely recognised deficiencies in NHS information. The task of the steering group was to define a common core of information for district management which could be aggregated for use at regional and DHSS level. According to the steering group, it was important to break the vicious circle of under-use of information and poor quality of the data collected. The steering group undertook a comprehensive and detailed review of the statistics available for health service management and drew up a minimum data set.

Management budgeting will help in respect of two key objectives in the Griffiths report. First, it will provide more useful financial information, clearly setting out who has incurred what expenditure; secondly, and more importantly, it will in the longer term create a much more cost-conscious professional staff, especially doctors, who are the initiators of all expenditure through their actions in respect of admission, treatment and discharge of patients. By involving professional staff, and giving them an incentive to use resources more efficiently and effectively, a greater volume and/or quality of patient care may be achieved.

Körner will help in producing information which is more relevant to assessing performance, and more appropriate to a proactive style of management.

Central initiatives

The review process

The review process, introduced in 1982, has also been one of major importance. At the Regional/DHSS review the meeting is chaired by the Secretary of State or a minister, and this annual meeting is used to assess the performance, both in general and specific terms, of the region as a whole. The minister meets with the chairman of the regional health authority, and both are accompanied by a number of professional advisers. Apart from a general review of financial performance and implementation of overall policy guidelines, for example a shift in the emphasis of care to the community, there is discussion on current issues applicable to all regions, such as the progress made towards the introduction of Körner. Other issues applicable to individual regions, for example, why a particular region has increased rather than reduced its management costs, are also discussed.

Each year there is a similar meeting between the RHA and each DHA with a similar spread of topics and representation of officers. Increasingly, DHA's are holding review meetings with unit management teams within the district, and some meetings include members of health authorities.

The purpose of all of these meetings is to review progress and to ensure, for example, that within a region there is a consistent and integrated approach to the pursuit of objectives and the provision of care. The danger which exists is that such meetings can be used to raise issues inappropriately, when they should be dealt with in another forum, or that the meetings are used to score points.

The principle of review meetings is sound. Care must, however, be taken to ensure that they are restricted to a few issues, of a policy nature, and that they do not deteriorate into petty arguments. They also form part of the communication process and, though the identification of key issues, help to shape strategic plans.

Rayner scrutinies

A number of Rayner scrutinies have been published. These are studies undertaken by NHS staff, specifically seconded for this purpose, on a wide range of subjects, for example:

- non-ambulance transport;
- non-emergency ambulance services;
- central stores policy;
- residential accommodation for staff;
- recruitment advertising;
- collection of income;
- cost of catering;
- collection of fees under the Road Traffic Act 1972;
- use of forms.

In each case, authorities have been required to review present arrangements with a view to reducing costs or increasing productivity. Some scrutinies, for example, residential accommodation for staff, have had a profound effect and caused much controversial debate, whilst others, for example, non-ambulance transport, have been the catalyst for

49

authorities to review their services with a much more commercial perspective. There has, however, been little exchange of information between authorities on the process of implementation, and it is too early to judge how effective any change will be.

Manpower

There have been a number of important developments in respect of staffing levels and training. During 1983 the DHSS laid down overall manpower limits for the NHS, and these limits were applied to regions and in turn to districts. For the first time there was a ceiling on the number of staff who could be in post at a given date (31st March) as well as a cash limit for an authority. This figure was made known to authorities part way through the financial year and created some difficulties; however, it was interesting to note that the reduction in manpower at 31st March was actually greater than that proposed by the DHSS. The introduction of manpower targets also attempted to control the number of staff in different categories by emphasising the importance of maintaining or increasing the number of staff directly providing patient care, and reducing those supporting this activity. Whilst this was successful to an extent, it may not have satisfied sufficiently the objectives of the centre. The competitive tendering exercise has however already brought about a reduction in the number of support staff.

The other important development in respect of manpower was the establishment of the NHS Training Authority. This body has the difficult task of co-ordinating a wide range of training activity which has been in existence for some time, and at the same time trying to cope with the new challenges of general management and all the training needs that this produced. Although much progress has been made in developing specific skills and changing the managerial environment, further work will be necessary to ensure that this progress is consolidated and that future challenges can be met.

Family Practitioner Committees

Family practitioner committees became autonomous bodies in April 1985. Whilst some would argue that this is a retrograde step and will increase the insular nature of the FPC, the requirement for FPC's and DHA's to collaborate over planning, cross representation of members, and political will should ensure that they are an integral part of the NHS. Current issues include internal efficiency, computerisation, and the nature of the service they provide; for example should they manage district nursing services?

A Green Paper on services provided by doctors and dentists has long been expected and may well produce considerable debate. An important question is whether 'health maintenance organisations' (HMOs) should be formed as a possible initiative to control costs and integrate primary and secondary care.

Information systems

The work of the NHS/DHSS steering group to produce recommendations on minimum data sets was referred to earlier. Information in the recommended formats (there were seven sub-groups, including clinical services, manpower and financial information) is to be collected with effect from April 1987. Most authorities are linking this initiative to the introduction of computerised patient administration systems. Ideally, all management information will ultimately be integrated and capable of responding to local managers' information requirements. The status of computers in the NHS has recently been raised by the formation of the Information Advisory group under the chairmanship of one of the directors of the NHS management board.

Performance indicators, now available in computerised form for use by local health managers, provide areas for further and often fruitful investigation, which may well lead to greater value for money and/or removal of pockets of unsatisfactory levels of care. The availability of these indicators has been received with mixed feelings; it remains to be seen whether they will provide a useful tool or be disregarded as they fail to reflect adequately the peculiarities of an organisation.

Supplies

There have been several reports on supplies in the NHS. Following the latest report, of the Supply Board Working Group in 1978, the Health Service Supply Council was established to develop policies and effect savings. This body was abolished in 1985 and its function taken over by the NHS management board. During the interim years, some progress was made in respect of the organisation of supplies departments, centralisation of purchasing and storage, and computerisation of systems.

Audit and efficiency

In 1983, a DHSS/NHS Audit Working Group, under the chairmanship of Mr. Patrick Salmon, recommended a more systematic approach to audit and the development of consortium arrangements between authorities. It also recommended the development of value for money studies, and some authorities have taken tentative steps to establish new departments.

The introduction of cost improvement programmes has required all authorities to initiate a wide-ranging examination of current services in order to release resources for direct patient care, especially in the fields of mental illness and mental handicap. At the same time, all authorities are required to test the efficiency of catering, domestic, and laundry services, and whilst some see this as a politically motivated initiative there is little doubt that substantial savings have been made and a more cost-conscious environment created.

Property and the works function

In 1983 the Ceri Davies Report on under-used and surplus property in the NHS was published. Authorities are required to look critically at the use of property (e.g. space utilisation, functional suitability) and to dispose of surplus property wherever possible. This exercise has been made even more important as a result of both the Rayner scrutiny on accommodation for staff and the closure of large institutions and the development of community care.

Conclusions

The NHS has had to adapt over the years to several different management arrangements. The concept of management teams and consensus management in 1974 was greeted by some with considerable hostility, and yet in 1985 many of these same people are reluctant to see the concept change.

It is inevitable that any government which wishes to maximise the use of resources will bring to the NHS, as to other public authorities, a new approach in respect of management and a vigorous approach to the achievement of value for money.

Whilst some would argue about the pace of change, or the method of achieving it, there can be no doubt that significant benefits have been achieved since 1980. The NHS is now much more orientated to objective setting, review of performance, achieving real efficiencies, and providing managers with the tools they need in terms of management and financial information. Changes in mangement structure and a concentration on previously untouched, yet high cost, areas have brought about a new, often very effective, environment.

The real test will come in three to five years time when the newly appointed general managers will have to demonstrate the progress achieved. If the momentum can be maintained, if there is a balance drawn between achievement of performance and sensitivity to patient needs, and if care is taken to listen to the views of consumers, then the NHS should be improved significantly. Whether momentum can be maintained, and whether general managers and authority members are able to distinguish the fine line between productivity and personal service remains to be seen.

Chapter 6

Information technology

A chapter on the impact of new technology on the public sector could easily become an overview of developments in the information technology (IT) industry generally. Much of what can be said about the effects of new technology is common to other parts of the economy, especially to the service and financial industries.

It is as true of the public sector as elsewhere that the benefits of new technology are not as readily achieved as some of the IT industry's more enthusiastic spokesmen would claim. In practice, the picture is a confused one, with rapid development in some quarters, unfulfilled expectations in others and elsewhere little evidence of change. Information systems and technology have a key role to play in the management of change—they offer opportunities for providing rapid, relevant information to all levels of management, which perhaps did not exist five years ago, and the very process of systems development allows an opportunity (regrettably not always grasped) to look carefully at how work is best organised and managed.

Four main topics have been chosen for this chapter. Through being selective, we are able to single out some themes that are of particular relevance to the public sector.

The four topics are:

- office information systems;
- new approaches to systems developments;
- data protection and security;
- the Alvey programme.

Office information systems

Phrases such as 'the paperless office', which abounded three or four years ago, are not heard so much nowadays. On the other hand, those who dismiss office technology as little more than word processing are being blind to the more fundamental changes now possible in working methods in the office.

As with so many other changes in the public sector, the pace of change is not uniform across the sector. Some of the reasons for the mixed response are:

- the technology is still developing rapidly; there is always a considerable lag between what can be demonstrated by a supplier and what is sufficiently robust to be successfully installed on site;
- natural human resistance to changes in working methods. Trade unions have demanded safeguards for their members in some organisations; in practice, this has not been a major constraint across much of the public sector;
- the investment required, which with general constraints on capital expenditure may be the decisive factor. Furthermore, the question of payback is often difficult to assess, particularly where quantifiable benefits are sought before the investment is made.

It is for all these reasons that the normal approach to office systems, and the accepted good practice, is to run a pilot office system in one part of the organisation. A pilot has the following benefits:

- alternative approaches can be tried without heavy investment in hardware or training;
- a demonstration can be provided of where the difficulties arise and how they can be overcome;
- it is normally acceptable for management to approve funds for a pilot without a quantifiable payback being identified in advance.

On a wider scale, a series of innovative office automation implementations have been undertaken in over 20 public sector organisations in the last two or three years, with funding assistance from the Department of Trade and Industry. A sub-group of the Computer Services Association has been responsible for project management and appraisal. As a member of this group, Peat Marwick has been responsible for two feasibility studies, including one in a county council, and has managed the implementation process for a district health authority.

The office automation pilots have been well documented, and the successes and failures analysed. The general experience has been that, whilst the authorities have been glad to have taken part, and feel that they have benefited from the experience, it is very hard to identify clear cost or efficiency benefits. The limitations identified by the pilots are both in the inability of the current technology to replace many tasks performed manually in the office, and in the attitudes of the staff using the equipment. In these respects, experience has been much the same in both public and private sectors.

Many public sector organisations are now considering their communications networks, and some are likely to invest heavily in new technology for both voice and data transmission. The potential in this area is exciting for public authorities, which often have a large number of operational and administrative sites spread over a wide area. Changes in the regulatory environment, especially in the areas of liberalisation of telecommunications and the effect on tariff structures of an increasingly competitive situation, provide both an opportunity and a responsibility to improve value for money.

The potential for external links is considerable, and can apply both to enabling the organisation to have electronic access to external services and databases, and to providing the public or external users with access to information an authority wishes to make available. The last point is particularly relevant to the needs of local authorities for publicising their own services and for providing a public viewdata information service, which a number of authorities have already done.

New approaches to systems developments

The Peat Marwick publication *Financial Management in the Public Sector 1979-1984* devotes a chapter to the use of packaged software, to meet the needs for new management accounting systems, emerging from the FMI and other pressures for better financial information. That chapter identifies the following key factors lying behind this change:

- the pressure for new systems to be developed quickly, without the pitfalls of excess costs or of unreliability that have occurred in the past;
- the availability of good quality applications packages;

- the increasing lead taken by users, rather than DP professionals, both in the design and implementation of systems.

Public sector organisations are large users of packaged software. The key application (in all sectors) has been the general ledger, to provide financial and management information, but there is a growing trend to implement other package-based financial systems such as purchase ledgers and asset management packages and personnel systems. Decision support systems (sophisticated modelling systems which can represent the effect of pursuing alternative policies) are also coming into use, but their use seems to be limited by the lack of sufficient quantifiable non-financial data to make full use of the technology available.

There are many more options available for systems development than in the past. Applications can be processed on microcomputers, minicomputers or mainframes, as integrated or non-integrated systems arranged on a centralised or distributed basis. Current and future information systems techniques and methodologies include database, fourth generation languages, prototyping and artificial intelligence (expert) systems.

Whilst there are always dangers in making generalisations, it is probably true to say that some of the newer techniques are not as widely used in the public sector as elsewhere. This may be partly a result of a wish to avoid untried methods at public expense, but it may also be a result of the excessive influence of data processing departments which wish to retain what they perceive as their position as controllers of the organisation's systems, and a natural resistance to change. The results of these attitudes can be frustration of the users, who may then seek their own solution at possibly greater expense.

The opportunities presented by information technology and the increasing expectations of users have made it increasingly important for organisations to have an IT strategy, and within that strategy a realistic implementation programme that recognises:

- priority areas for the application of IT in terms of service improvement or cost reduction;
- the financial investment the body is able to make;
- managerial commitment in the departments affected;
- the availability of training resources;
- any industrial relations issues;

57

- the availability of reliable technology;
- the desirability of tight but achievable timescales.

Many new systems developments are less than satisfactory because due consideration has not been given to one or more of these factors.

An example of a part of the public sector which is trying to make great strides at present is the NHS, which has tended to lag behind in computer developments in the past. NHS computing has often been characterised by:

- dominance of regional mainframe computers;
- extensive influence of central committees on systems design and developments;
- insufficient competition amongst suppliers.

Much is now changing in the health service, and a period of major investment in systems for patient administration, management budgeting, personnel management and supplies is beginning. The background to these changes is described in Chapter 5, with particular impetus coming from the Körner report.

The programmes of development that are now being planned for several NHS regions are exciting and ambitious. With the general shortage of IT skills in all sectors of the economy being particularly acute in the public sector, for reasons which have much to do with relative levels of remuneration, but which may also relate to job satisfaction, heavy demands will be placed on management to implement the systems successfully.

Data protection and security

The Data Protection Act 1984 has heightened awareness of an aspect of information technology that has not always been given the highest priority in the public sector.

It is the first piece of legislation in the United Kingdom to address the use of computers and it reflects increasing public concern about the potential misuse of the power of computers. Computers can now store and analyse vast amounts of data. With sopisticated communication systems, data can be transferred to distant locations and across international boundaries.

The Act gives new rights to data subjects, that is individuals who are the subject of personal data. Personal data is information which identifies directly or indirectly a living individual and can be automatically processed. The Act also imposes responsibilities and liabilities on data users. As major users of computer data, public sector bodies are clearly very much affected by the Act.

Broadly the data protection principles state that personal data shall:

- be collected and processed fairly and lawfully;
- be held only for specified, lawful and registered purposes;
- be used only for registered purposes or disclosed to registered recipients;
- be adequate and relevant to the purpose for which they are held;
- be accurate, and where necessary kept up-to-date;
- be held no longer than is necessary for the stated purpose;
- have appropriate security surrounding them.

The principles also state the right of individuals to have access to data held about themselves.

Unless data users can claim an exemption they will have to register the purpose or purposes for which they hold personal data, the type of individuals this covers, general description of the type of personal data, the source of the data, who will have access to it and the countries outside the UK to which data may be transferred. (Most of the exemptions are accompanied by provisos or limitations and they must be examined carefully before a data user concludes that any of them apply to him.)

The register provides individuals with the names and addresses of data users processing personal data, and details of the nature, source and use of the data. Via the register, individuals will be entitled to ask data users whether they are the subject of personal data held by them, and if so, to be supplied with copies of that data.

In other countries where similar legislation already exists the level of subject access requests has been very low. However, the public sector will probably have more than their fair share of access requests as the interest will relate directly to the sensitivity of data.

The Act provides for a phased implementation introducing first those provisions for which little or no preparation is required. The first provisions were effective from 12th September 1984. The remainder come into effect during a two year timetable commencing on the appointed day, 11th November 1985, which is the date when registration commenced.

The amount of work necessary in preparing for registration and compliance with the other requirements of the Act should not be underestimated. It has been suggested that local authorities and public bodies could face costs of £9m to £11m for the first two years, while Government departments are likely to spend £5.5m implementing the Act.

To respond to the Act, public sector organisations need to undertake a detailed survey to establish whether registration is appropriate and, if so, to provide the necessary information for registration. Such a survey can also provide other benefits; for example, it can be used to compile an inventory of computer equipment and may represent an opportunity to reconsider the overall strategy for computing.

The Act has been designed to try to cope with the ways in which personal data may be used in the future. To avoid being dated by the introduction of new technology the Act has concentrated on the uses to which data may be put, rather than on the equipment which is used.

Only the future will tell whether the legislation has met the prime objective of reassuring the individual citizen that computers can be used without risk of abuse. We await with interest the Registrar's annual report to each House of Parliament and the outcome of the court cases raised by individuals claiming for damage and distress under the provisions of this new legislation.

Looking beyond the Data Protection Act, there are a number of other important aspects of data protection and security.

A disruption or misuse of the computer service can lead to operational disruption, cause considerable embarrassment and involve serious financial loss. As well as the dangers of theft or fraud, there are risks such as:

- loss of confidentiality of information;
- actual loss of information, both accidental and otherwise;
- inability to maintain continuity of processing following various types of system failure;
- unauthorised modification of information;
- failure to maintain prudent standards of system development, operation and maintenance.

Relatively little information is available to public authorities about the extent of these risks, and what their potential impact is. The increasing dependence of organisations on IT to control their operations indicates that a major breakdown could have a dire impact.

Another aspect of security is disaster recovery planning, which enables an organisation to recover with minimum disruption from the effects of a disaster—accidental or deliberate—affecting a computer installation. It is the experience of Peat Marwick that many public sector organisations have given only limited thought to these matters and their possible consequences.

The Alvey programme

The government announced its decision to implement the report of the Alvey Committee on 23rd April 1983. The Alvey programme is the UK government's response to Japanese and American efforts in IT, directed at the so-called 'fifth generation' of computers. Much has happened since then, with the push towards co-operative ventures in information technology (IT) research.

The Alvey Directorate itself is frequently referred to as just such an example of co-operation. It is staffed by people from the Department of Trade and Industry, the Ministry of Defence, the Science and Engineering Research Council and the universities. Companies from the private sector have also seconded staff to the Directorate and many people throughout the IT industry have contributed to the launch of Alvey.

A glance at the Alvey Directorate's Report indicates some trends in the way in which IT innovation is being directed. The report deals with work on large demonstrator projects, infrastructure and communications, man-machine interface, very large scale integration (VLSI), software engineering and intelligent knowledge based systems (IKBS) or 'expert systems'.

The list of projects for IKBS technology is of particular interest. Some 36 schemes have been approved, with a substantial involvement in these schemes from academic with 12 universities and two polytechnics being beneficiaries of Alvey funding. Innovative work is clearly flourishing in this part of the public community, with some significant progress at the theoretical and experimental levels.

However, the potential users of this new technology are less in evidence. If we accept the claims of the IKBS experts, the technology is about to revolutionise many areas of business and commerce. Systems for advising on tax and insurance are propounded for the financial sector. Applications in fault diagnosis, training and counselling are expected for engineering and professional services. The Alvey demonstration project for the DHSS will involve incorporating knowledge of Social Services benefit rules in an IKBS. However, while the business community is threatened with revolution, public sector users (other than the DHSS) do not appear to have taken much interest in the potential of this technology. Importantly for the public sector at large, IKBS systems are thought to have a role in the interpretation of legislation.

It is probably true that public sector organisations are generally reluctant to experiment with new techniques until they can see evidence of practical application. It is not clear whether this is evidence of absence of management interest, a lack of awareness, or simply a reflection that the claims of academics are ahead of their time.

Two important Alvey initiatives in IKBS awareness have been launched. The ALFEX club (Alvey financial information exchange), of which Peat Marwick is a founder member, is a consortium of leading financial institutions. The consortium is concerned with applying IKBS technology to the financial appraisal of company viability. This initiative has shown that the financial services sector wish to be in from the start of innovation in IKBS technology. The PLANIT club, of which Peat Marwick is also a founder member, is developing the application of knowledge engineering technology to project planning. This is a consortium of leading manufacturing organisations, academic institutions and management consultants. These initiatives are indicative of a high level of commercial interest in innovation through IKBS, or expert systems, albeit still at an experimental stage. The applications being developed have obvious relevance to the public sector.

It is possible that the use of expert systems will become a reality in the public sector before long. In every organisation there are key staff whose skills and experience are referred to by junior staff. Expert systems would allow this wisdom and knowledge to be tapped more efficiently and effectively. For example, in the field of housing benefits the complicated rules are probably only fully understood by one or two people in a local authority. The ability to make this knowledge and the expert interpretation available to all staff who have to advise the public would increase the quality of the service given, as well as giving the key staff more time to devote to creative tasks as more decisions are able to be made by junior staff.

Conclusions

Government has often been accused of not having a consistent policy towards the high technology industries, and towards education and training in new technology. There certainly seems to be little doubt that the UK, and Europe as a whole, is falling behind other countries such as Japan and the USA. These are broad issues beyond the scope of this review.

Within the public sector itself the picture is mixed. There are examples of bold experimentation and of beneficial uses of information technology but there is also a shortage of funds or an unwillingness to invest in information technology. In the long term, however, the greatest constraints are likely to be the shortage of IT skills and a lack of willingness to use IT.

Some other Peat Marwick publications

Financial management in the public sector: a review 1979-84

Management information and control in Whitehall—proceedings of a seminar (jointly with RIPA)

Developing the FMI: changes in process and culture—proceedings of a seminar (jointly with RIPA)

Policy management and policy assessment—proceedings of a seminar (jointly with RIPA)

Personnel policies and the management of change

Finance for new projects in the UK—a guide to private and public sector initiatives and grants (also available on-line)